Leveling up

with

GUSTO!

*A Roadmap to Sustaining
a Profitable Showroom*

DEBORAH FLATE

Dialogue
consulting

Table of Contents

"I had to make my own living and my own opportunity. But I made it! Don't sit down and wait for the opportunities to come. Get up and make them."

-Madam C.J. Walker

This is exactly why I do what I do — these are the results I want for every client and/or business I work with!

Dear Deborah,

I want express my gratitude for the excellent work that you have done in helping me grow my sales. Working with you has been an absolute joy, and I am thrilled with the results that we have achieved together.

Before partnering with your company, I was struggling to achieve the level of sales and sale strategy that I desired for my team. However, after working with you, we have been able to see an increase in sales, and we are often left wondering why we haven't been doing this all along. You have encouraged us to be more mindful regarding our sales strategy, to ask more qualifying questions and to be more deliberate in the selections we offer to our clients.

The strategies and tactics that you have provided have been incredibly valuable, and we have seen immediate results. Deborah has been a pleasure to work with, and your expertise and guidance have been instrumental in our success.

I would highly recommend your company to anyone who is looking to grow their sales and take their business to the next level. Thank you for your exceptional work, and I look forward to continuing our partnership.

All the best,

Brenda Westphal
Owner

I want to begin this journey with you by sharing how much I love the interior design industry. I've now spent almost half my life as a designer, salesperson, regional sales director, national sales director, and now as a business owner and consultant helping product companies, showrooms and sales teams in the design industry to level up their current way of doing business.

This book will show you that there is a reason for the adage: **work smarter, not harder**. Here's another way to look at it: **busyness does not equal business**. I believe working in the same manner as we did when I was a salesperson back in the late '80s through the early 2000s is working very hard with disappointing and inconsistent results. I have found that most showrooms I work with are unfortunately still stuck in that era. They are struggling now more than ever, and sadly many of them have closed their doors.

If you are responsible for running a showroom or product company, please ask yourself:

- Are you losing good employees?
- Are you finding it difficult to find good employees?
- Are your sales inconsistent?
- Do you look at your Profits and Loss Statement (P&L) with uncertainty?
- Do you think you need to cut costs?
- Are your sales at the mercy of the momentum of the economy, a product line, or the "busyness" of design firms?

If you answered yes to any of these questions, this book is for you.

Using my industry knowledge and experience from the past 35 years, I provide a roadmap for running a successful showroom business. It's for showrooms and product companies represented in showrooms who want to see a turnaround and more profitability. In addition to strategies for reimagining the showroom as a sales organization, it also aims to help showrooms give interior designers more of what they want.

This book aims to provide insights, strategies, and examples to help businesses modernize their practices, overcome challenges, and thrive in the current market landscape. It is meant to offer practical advice on leveraging technology, optimizing workflows, and adopting innovative sales and marketing techniques to achieve sustainable growth.

I've participated in several roundtable discussions with very established designers and the resounding consensus is that the most important part of working with a seller is service. "OK," you say, "we do that in spades." But do you?

We must ask ourselves: *How* are we servicing our clients and are they still best practices? Or are we stuck in old ways that no longer serve us *or* our designers?

My Track Record

While working with countless sellers and showrooms, I have had some colossal successes and even some failures. I've learned from both, and think I have a good grasp of what works and what doesn't.

I started my own journey with a degree in Interior Architecture. After five years of doing commercial and hospitality design, I decided I wanted to go in a different direction that was still in the industry I loved. That's when I began an 18-year career in outside sales and management, where I was able to both increase sales and decrease operating expenses (OpEx) for three major, multi-line, high-end showrooms.

My selling career was primarily in the Architecture and Design (A&D) commercial sector with some residential sales, too. I was considered a top performer and worked really hard. In retrospect, I may have been working harder, and not always smarter.

At two of the three showrooms, I was a Regional Sales Director and oversaw a 13 state territory. With the right strategies I turned them both from struggling showrooms to hugely successful profit centers without making any cuts. Instead I actually hired support people who helped generate even more sales.

In 2001 I started my own firm, Dialogue Consulting, which provides sales training and consulting services to showroom businesses and product companies. Initially I was hired by two companies as their National Sales Director. Charged with the task of growing sales, I'm proud to say I was able to do so— exponentially.

I have since helped numerous showroom businesses and salespeople go from floundering to flourishing, from underperforming to profitable by learning how to sell more efficiently with my Master Sales Course and GUSTO© system. The key is to develop and implement the right strategies to increase sales and lower OpEx… and now I want to help you do the same!

The Hard Truths

The industry must take a hard look at how the landscape has changed. If we don't face reality and, more importantly, make changes to our business model, more showrooms will struggle and be forced to close.

First, let's take a look at some facts about the industry which we must accept, like it or not:

- Today many design centers are either currently in or have been in foreclosure.
- Industry icons such as Donghia, Robert Allen, J. Robert Scott, and Dessin Fournir are just a few of the showroom organizations that have closed over the past five years. I predict there will be more in the next five years.
- Many designers charge their clients a markup, putting an additional charge up to 50% of the sale price on products their clients buy. This business model is making it more and more difficult for salespeople to sell high-end, expensive products because designers cannot sell it at the even higher, marked up price.
- Some experienced designers are "aging" out of the industry and many newer designers operate differently. It's imperative for showrooms to strike a balance between existing and new ways of doing business.
- When I worked in sales during the 1990s through the early 2000s, my ONLY competitors were housed in other design centers. I only competed with companies and showrooms that sold to the trade. This is no longer true! The landscape has completely changed today, with more companies vying for that elusive sale.

- The Covid-19 pandemic caused tectonic changes to the marketplace and business. The old business model of designers dropping into a showroom or seeing designers in their firms and meeting with librarians and designers regularly, has dramatically changed, and I believe will never go back to what it once was.

So how do we break through all these challenges and ensure our showrooms or product companies don't meet the same fate as some of the iconic companies which closed their doors?

Let's consider the options…

We can wait and see what happens, and continue to be at the whim of design firms' way of doing business. (No!)

We can continue to hold on to old beliefs thinking this ship will, someday, right itself and people will adapt to our way of thinking. (No!)

OR

We can thoughtfully reflect on our practices, take initiative, and adjust our business model to meet these new and everlasting changes. To me, this is the *only* path to take.

Even though things might seem bleak or fatalistic, we can turn things around!

We must first ask: How did we get here? Why are showrooms on the decline?

Simply put, *showrooms need to get with the times*. Showrooms have pretty much been doing the same things for the past FIFTY years.

They have failed to adapt and evolve, and the consequences have been dire.

This book will explain the pitfalls of sticking to the status quo and teach you the most important changes you should make to create profitable showrooms.

Here I outline seven critical ways that showrooms are stuck in the past, and seven proven strategies to improve operations and boost sales.

7 Reasons Showrooms are Struggling | 7 Solutions to Turn Things Around

"Approach Each Customer
With The Idea Of Helping Him
Or Her To Solve A Problem Or
Achieve A Goal, Not Of Selling
A Product Or Service."

-Brian Tracy

1

Showroom Managers and Salespeople focus too much on *"Showing"* product instead of treating the showroom like a Sales Organization.

Traditionally, showrooms operate with a "build it, and they will come" mindset. After years of research, involvement with showrooms, and successfully turning struggling showrooms into big profit centers, I am blowing the lid off showrooms and saying that these principles no longer work today.

Most showrooms are stuck thinking that spending most of the showroom budget on the design of the space will enhance their branding, entice designers to enter, and generate sales. That just doesn't work anymore. It never really worked, but prior to 2009, we fooled ourselves into believing the economy would remain strong, there would not be the competition there is today, and there would be no need for a change.

We now see that we were mistaken in thinking clients would keep buying luxury products exclusively through showrooms.

Much of the luxury design business was built on cache and exclusivity. Therefore it seemed logical to keep the design centers and product availability exclusive. The economy was strong, people were less budget-conscious, less product was obtainable, and that's what the design business was built on.

That business model is now flawed and no longer works!

What worked 10 or 20 years ago does not work today. The evidence is abundant.

Now design centers are being turned over to non-design, high-tech companies. Major lines are leaving showrooms because of low performance, and many showrooms are going out of business. Major product companies are moving out of design centers and into independent ground-level spaces, which further depletes the needed income for those design centers. Others are "hanging on by a thread" while looking for solutions, most of which have proven ineffective.

The "good old days" of having a visually beautiful showroom and designers using them on a consistent basis as the main generator of sales were only as effective as the company's momentum and ease of business. But, today this is outdated thinking. Hence the cliché "good OLD days." We now can see that this philosophy was all built on a house of cards and false assumptions that things would remain the same forever.

Back in the 1990s and 2000s, it was common for 20-30 designers to visit a design center daily. That is just not happening anymore. With the advent of so many ways of communication, today's designers can get products and even samples from multiple sources, which further bites into our client-facing opportunities.

And many of those designers had clients who only wanted "the best." Back then, it was rare for those clients to purchase retail, and online opportunities did not exist.

We have kept the same definition of to-the-trade; however, many end users have redefined luxury. They may not even use a designer; if they do, they may not spend luxury showroom prices.

Unfortunately, we can now see that this way of thinking needs to be fixed since showrooms are still struggling and closing.

> ## That business model has now collapsed, and we will never recover unless we change how we do business.

Too many showroom owners think success is about having more beautiful products and spending tens of thousands, even millions, of dollars to produce a beautiful showroom. If it's a multi-line showroom, most represented product companies are led to believe the same philosophy and they keep providing more and more new products.

Sure, showroom sales skyrocketed after Covid-19 lockdowns lifted and home improvement projects could resume. The economy has gotten stronger and home sales are up today. But let's not fool ourselves into thinking this is sustainable. Just like other bubbles, we are now witnessing the post-pandemic slowdown. We need a more sustainable approach.

Product companies are looking for that band-aid that will bolster sales. They're trying to create the next great, beautiful, or functional product. They are grasping at what they think will improve the bottom line for the showrooms in which they are represented.

However, this approach produces thousands of dollars in product, time spent by the showroom staff, and even construction to add a new line or to give the showroom a "new" look.

Salespeople are struggling to get appointments with designers, so the cry for NEW NEW NEW is deafening. They believe that they must show designers new products in order to sell more. This is just not true! In most cases, less really *can be* more!

To keep this industry thriving, we must change what we are doing and how we think about a showroom's function.

"I've learned that people will forget what you said, people will forget what you did, but people will never forget how you made them feel."

-Maya Angelou

SOLUTION:

Focus more on the salesperson and less on the product.

After years of experience in the showroom business and interviewing hundreds of designers, one of the most important things designers look for in showrooms is highly trained, proactive, responsive, and well-informed showroom employees to make their jobs easier! Although it's obvious that the product is what you sell, if you don't have well-trained salespeople, the product does not matter.

Salespeople need to *create* sales, and they make sales when they find the right accounts and build a long lasting relationship with those accounts. It's not the tearsheet, Instagram page, or even the most stunning showroom that makes a purchase order.

While we are a visual industry and designers look to us for inspiration and trends, our marketing alone does not sustain or increase sales. Sales are the only thing to sustain any business and lead to increased profitability. Therefore our thinking has to be repositioned: If our sales approach is not reimagined and strengthened, no amount of beautiful product or showroom designs will improve the bottom line, get more designers in showrooms, or get salespeople more accounts.

The answer is not bringing in more products, but instead investing resources to change the landscape of today's modern showroom. It's much more important to invest in highly trained sales managers and salespeople than in more and more products. The GUSTO system I use does just that. It results in highly trained and effective salespeople.

Designers rarely, if ever, base their buying solely on products. And the social distancing protocols during the Covid pandemic exacerbated the need for salespeople and showroom personnel to be an extension of their design firms.

In general, a showroom is like any other business. It needs a strong strategic plan and an effective sales and management force. Think of it this way: It's not simply a showroom with products to impress designers; it's a SALES ORGANIZATION that has chosen to sell beautiful product.

I sold beautiful product throughout my entire career. But working with beautiful things was just a bonus. I could have been selling paper clips. The sales approach was always the top priority. If it's not the top priority in your showroom, that's what needs to change *right now.*

CASE STUDY

I was the regional sales director for two major, luxury showrooms. After years of both showrooms not being profitable, I turned both around to profitability in a year. My "secret" was not to think of these showrooms as a place for beautiful products, but as a sales organization that happened to sell beautiful products. But the strategy remained like any other Fortune 100 company.

I implemented a strategic plan to ensure the entire staff was selling directly or supporting the sales effort. I made changes that prevented salespeople from being enslaved by useless paperwork. Instead they were empowered to focus 100% of their efforts on selling.

Without a single cut or layoff, I increased sales by over $2 million for one showroom and $5.5 million for the other.

"Value The Relationship More Than The Quota."

-Jeff Gitomer

2

Showrooms are only measuring whether salespeople are meeting their sales goals.

During my 18-plus years in showrooms as both an outside salesperson and a manager, we always had sales goals. What I noticed was that the sales process needed to be taught and the measurement of success needed to be revised.

You're probably thinking, "But we always have had sales goals." This may be true, but you must go deeper than sales goals. Sales goals are not a measurement of the sales process, but a result. Yes, the success or failure in meeting sales goals is a measurement; however, you are only measuring the results of the sales process if you only measure sales goals. ***I call this only looking at "top-line."*** It's not a way to measure the effectiveness of a salesperson. After all, do all your salespeople meet their goals every month? If not, what results are you measuring, and more importantly, what is the solution to making them steadier?

Many salespeople will tell me who their "top accounts" are and therefore spend a lot of time with these accounts. When I review their sales figures, often these design firms buy erratically based on their business at that time. They may have two big projects a year and those sales add up at the end of the year. This is what looking at "top line" sales is. However, when those firms are not specifying and salespeople still focus their time on showing more and more products to those firms, where does the business come from when they are not specifying products? This illustrates how vulnerable sales can be.

In addition to sales "top-line" sales results, we need to look at loyalty from clients and get sellers to lean into these clients more often. Consistent business forms a solid book of business that's less vulnerable to outside influences such as the economy, interest rates, Wall Street, or any pandemic.

Knowledge is power, and so is finding the right client.

If salespeople are not coached or taught to embrace the whole ***sales process and find those clients who have consistent business,*** they may or may not meet those goals, and the result is that they are very vulnerable to competition and any fluctuation in the economy. Looking at "top-line" sales is often a haphazard way of approaching a showroom's success, and why many showrooms suffer from inconsistent sales and low profitability.

When salespeople do not fully understand a new sales process, they tend to gauge the value of a client by how busy the client is, how often they come into the showroom, how well-known they are in the industry, and by the number of quotes they request from their showroom. However, this is a completely flawed approach to sales strategies.

Owners of showrooms often ask me to train their salespeople to "close more quotes," thinking this will increase sales. I always respond that this shouldn't be the goal. What I actually need to teach them is 1) how to find the right client who specifies their needs to the salesperson, and 2) how to supply that client with product that exactly fits those needs. Only this will generate more consistent business for the salesperson.

In many instances, designers will add more work to the seller, who— if not properly trained and knowledgeable about sales processes— will fall victim to their unreasonable or incomplete requests. Times have changed from relying on in-depth, in-person conversations in the showroom to get a good grasp of how to satisfy a designer's needs. These days, emails and texts from designers can be quick, easy, and efficient, but they very often lead to more busywork for the seller. Designers might ask the seller to find something for them, without providing enough detailed information, that may not ultimately result in a sale. If the seller is not savvy and fails to utilize sales strategies, they won't know how to follow up and ask the right questions to get the necessary, detailed information that will help them actually make the sale. Simply put, lack of proper training to learn effective sales strategies results in inconsistent sales and a lot of wasted time.

In addition, failure to implement a sales plan and training often means that sales become dependent on the momentum of a design firm. If the design firm needs a showroom product and thinks of a particular showroom, they contact the showroom and may buy a product. The inherent problem is that designers (like most humans) are creatures of habit. They typically like to work with the same product line, showroom, or seller over and over again, and continue to give that business to them. If you're not part of a loyal relationship and *facilitating the decision* with a "habitual" client, then you are missing out on sales.

"If You Are Not Moving Closer To What You Want In Sales (Or In Life), You Probably Aren't Doing Enough Asking."

-Jack Canfield

SOLUTION:

Establish a sales process, train salespeople on that process, and measure accountability.

To measure a salesperson's effectiveness, they must be properly trained on the sales process–not only the product–to ensure that they transform them into effective salespeople, not just "quote machines" and "order takers" or product presenters.

Salespeople are solely responsible
for growing the business; that's their
job.

There has to be a sales strategy. We need to teach them to "lean into loyalty." Find business by asking, asking, asking and finding out if they are the right fit for your products on a consistent basis. They need to target and focus on designers with monthly needs that can benefit from the product(s) sold by the showroom. They should know the value of their products, have clients who want that value, and those who have the budget to support their efforts. I call these strategic accounts where sellers should be aware of the buying cycle of all these strategic accounts.

CASE STUDY

I learned this lesson of needing a clear sales plan and process as a regional manager for a major multi-line showroom. During a sales meeting, I asked each of my salespeople to define the dollar number indicating a top account and to list the clients they believed were top accounts.

I then asked them to check the records and to add up three-month's worth of sales for these top accounts. I used that amount to generate projected yearly sales for these accounts.

Of the three salespeople and ten accounts per person, not one account measured up to what they defined as a top account. Not one! In some cases, the sales were so low that the salespeople were shocked. They had no idea that these designers were not buying and spending more.

This showroom needed a sales plan and better accountability. When I implemented the sales process GUSTO©, an entire system of measuring success, to determine the real top clients and train salespeople to allocate their time better, the sales increased almost immediately. After implementing this sales plan, the showroom consistently increased its sales and profitability after many unprofitable years.

Salespeople began to see how changing their old ways and looking to the right strategies could earn them more money. I also benefited by keeping these sellers happy, and they stayed with the company for a very long time.

Notes

"The price of doing the same old thing is far higher than the price of change."

-Bill Clinton

3

Salespeople are still selling the same way they did before online and retail became legitimate competitors.

Who hasn't bought a product online or in retail? Before the recession, this was thought of as difficult or low-brow. Nothing matched the cache and quality of the product that designers could get from a showroom.

This way of thinking has completely changed, affecting our business.

Today, technology has come full circle. Almost everything is available online or in retail, and clients and designers are much more comfortable ordering from these resources.

Ordering online offers some degree of immediate gratification to designer's clients. It's also a great way for designers (and their clients) to research from the comfort of their offices or homes. As a result, designers spend less time at design centers.

Retail often proves to be easier to sell to designers' clients! In today's business, that's a value to designers. Add to this, clients are savvier and well-traveled. They see and read about what's out there. Even shelter magazines are highlighting more retail products in both advertising and installations. The lines are blurring more and more every day.

Well-known designers who, in the past, would turn their noses up at retail are now purchasing retail. Clients observe this, making the retail market much more acceptable as a source of product. Just consider Restoration Hardware, which is now boasting that 40% of its sales are to-the-trade. Last year their sales were 6.1 BILLION dollars. Do you think some showrooms sales are being lost? You bet they are.

Retail is targeting and marketing to designers and that elusive HENRY (High Earners, Not Rich Yet) client. The product has become more sophisticated in design. Retail prices are increasing, but they still stay below showroom pricing.

Additionally, well-known product designers now sell and design for retail, making the "luxury" look more affordable and accessible.

Today it's become almost impossible for the average person (or even some designers) to discern the differences between retail products and products that are only sold to-the-trade. A designer's client *really* needs to see the difference between a retail sofa for $2,500 and a customized sofa for $10,000 from a showroom and the salesperson must justify why the product with the higher price tag fits the client's needs better.

In the past, the exclusiveness was a selling point. Today, if the client cannot discern the quality from the price, the salesperson is wasting time.

If a salesperson fails to qualify a sale effectively, (what's important to the client) this causes an extraordinary amount of work with no guaranteed result. It leads to fruitless back and forth, lost time, and ultimately a lost sale. And designers may have to, at times, acquiesce to the client's wishes. Justifying such huge price differences takes exceptional sales skills, which unfortunately, most designers have not developed.

Designers, by their very nature, want to design. They want to think of themselves as something other than salespeople. Although selling skills would certainly help their business, most designers just do not see that job role in their business paradigm. Therefore, it's entirely up to the showroom salesperson to identify how their product fits the client's needs and then sell that product effectively.

SOLUTION:

Salespeople need advanced sales training to compete with the current status of interior design product sales.

This is a crossroads in the interior design industry. Showrooms are searching for solutions and applying band-aids to the problems, falsely believing that the economy will come back and things will all be as they were pre-2009. Or continuing to think exclusivity and product will generate sales. The economy has returned from our great recession, but it has resulted in more and more product vying for a shrinking sector of the design industry and these old showroom strategies will NOT work in the 21st-century, post-Covid design market.

Showrooms continue to work in an analogue world, continuing to use old ways of business like an old IBM computer tower. We have to step into the future and think about what we can change to meet that challenge.

We can continue believing that old strategies will work, put our heads in the sand, and not look at reality. We can fool ourselves into thinking our showrooms are busy and clients continue to only buy product from these showrooms; *but in truth they are not and it's a false belief.* More is needed to increase sales, generate profitability, and form strong sales organizations.

We need to understand that the showroom business model has to change, and the only way we can sustain to-the-trade showrooms is to provide value. Value is not always defined by dollars.

> Value is defined by the designer's
> experience, which means making
> their job easier.

It's no longer enough to allow the business to come to us. We need to have our sales staff become more proactive. If a showroom does not have an outside program, it's time to implement one. If it does have one, it needs to focus less on product and more on finding business through targeting the right clients.

When clients come into the showroom, we must train our salespeople to act as salespeople and sell. It's no longer enough just to serve a client.

Notes

"The greatest leader is not necessarily the one who does the greatest things. He is the one that gets the people to do the greatest things."

-Ronald Reagan

4

Showroom managers function more like administrators than leaders.

Managers in design showrooms are thought of as administrators carrying out corporate policy. They ensure the showroom runs smoothly and the employees adhere to the policy. They are often considered part of the sales team rather than leaders, trainers, and motivators.

Administrative tasks begin to gradually take up more and more time, and the more time they spend on those tasks, the less time is spent focusing on analyzing, training, motivating, and leading. That's when company revenues and profits flat-line or start to decrease. And while many managers come from a sales background and often have excellent sales skills, they are typically not included in forming sales strategies (that is, if these even exist in the showroom) and, often, are not skilled trainers.

Showroom managers' responsibilities are typically those of a human resource planner and maintaining the looks and everyday functioning of the showroom. In addition, if the showroom manager is preparing for a major conference, this takes weeks of planning and executing *away* from daily operations. What they need to be doing is training and monitoring their salespeople to ensure they are making sales.

Rarely, if ever, is a showroom manager responsible for planning and implementing a REAL sales strategy that builds profitability. When showrooms look for a showroom manager, they want them to have sharply honed administrative qualities since they think those skills are necessary to run a successful showroom. The showroom manager's role inevitably turns into a clerical position.

Meanwhile, as managers become more administrative, their showrooms face decreasing customer frequency and employ confused and under-motivated sales staff. The result has a direct impact on performance and profitability.

Time and time again, the clients are disappointed with the sales teams: "You would think they would take the initiative to contact clients to see what's going on." Then what happens to those salespeople? They are criticized and left to do better or try harder. Or managers will admonish them for not selling enough. A struggling salesperson is either left to figure it out for themselves or often quit or is just fired and replaced with another salesperson that managers hope will do better.

Instead of motivating their sales staff, training them on the sales process, and coaching them to do better, managers often just *hope* that a salesperson will sell more. "They are salespeople; they should know better" is a common thought I consistently hear.

But hope is never a strategy!

What the salespeople need is real training on a real sales process. Sellers are often told WHAT, but rarely HOW to sell. They are told to increase sales, but need to know HOW to increase sales. So, without this knowledge and skills, the seller (myself included when I was in sales) just tries to work faster, get more samples to clients, and make more calls. MORE, MORE, MORE… yet, all too often, it gets them nowhere.

This happened to me during my sales career. I was never taught the HOW, so I went faster in my hamster wheel. I made more calls, generated as many quotes as possible, gave out even more samples, and connected with any firm with the word "design" in the title with no qualifications. And then stood back and prayed and hoped the sales would come through. Although the sad truth is I believed, as many sellers and managers continue to believe, this was the way to increase sales.

Most managers themselves need more understanding of the sales process. They, in turn, must also teach salespeople how to boost sales, and they must become critical when salespeople perform poorly.

You will not notice if mistakes are made during the selling process. It only shows up when sales are low, which is far too late. Suppose salespeople don't approach the right client with the correct strategy for making a sale or miss out because they are too busy with non-sales activity. Or perhaps they fail to uncover the client's current needs, so they don't expose them to as many solutions as possible. In that case, the manager may not even notice what the salesperson is doing wrong. Or worse yet, a manager might not even consider sales techniques as the problem.

Research shows that hiring a new employee costs the company an average of $115,000, with time and resources stolen from operating the business and instead devoted to completing the recruitment and hiring process and training new employees to get them up to speed. This is the "invisible" profit killer, which could be avoided with sound management leadership.

SOLUTION:

Sales Managers Must Function As Coaches Who Monitor Strategy And Hold Their Team Members Accountable.

Managers need to be thought of as sales managers. They should be thought of as leaders who train, coach, and oversee the profitability of the showroom. However, their responsibilities go much deeper than just monitoring sales goals.

Using a sports analogy, winning teams owe much of their success to ongoing coaching. They go out with a strategy, a way to execute it, and a system of measurement that goes beyond points or wins. The skills are taught, monitored, and consistently coached to do better. Even basketball legend Michael Jordan had Coach Phil Jackson to guide him to win, not just to get points, and that took strategy. That's why they were SIX time NBA champions!

We must think of a showroom manager as the coach of the sales floor, helping the sales team to victory. The managers must be qualified and empowered to be that coach. They must also develop and implement a sales plan. Following and monitoring a sales plan is integral to evaluating salespeople, coaching them on the process, and motivating them to perform better. Guardians of sales processes.

Revamping the sales manager role is an important part of changing how showrooms function, moving beyond the importance of aesthetics. When a capable sales manager implements and monitors a strong sales plan, the showroom becomes a true sales organization with the ability to make greater profits.

"I have been impressed with the urgency of doing. Knowing is not enough; we must apply. Being willing is not enough; we must do."

-Leonardo da Vinci

5

Sales training usually teaches knowledge rather than how to change behavior patterns. *Knowing* something does not necessarily mean you will be able to *do* something.

Some sales training or motivational presentations are often considered the "miracle pill" administered once, and management quietly waits for results. Often management is not even included in the training, and they are not expected to make any changes to their own practices. The training often involves talking about skills but fails to include any real-time experience or specific, measurable goals for the employees to meet. Salespeople are then instructed to start implementing new skills, but without enough specifics to actually put them into practice in meaningful ways.

They are given the WHAT, but not
the HOW.

The sales staff is often given ideas but needs more time or reinforcement to internalize these new ideas. Handouts are given, or emails are sent out and put away, and behavior patterns remain the same. An occasional sales meeting may be part of a showroom plan, but sales training and coming up with a sales plan are rarely a part of that meeting. Most of the focus is on current business, what closed, or what quotes have been generated. Managers may talk about low-producing lines with no follow-up.

And even if a sales trainer or motivator is brought in (and that is rare), they often have yet to live the showroom experience. They all have great theoretical knowledge but need more up-to-date experience or methods that fit our industry's current climate.

If people are taught to improve on a skill and then left on their own, they would, most likely, slip into old habits because it's always more comfortable! It's almost like muscle memory. It takes constant monitoring and to implement a new sales strategy and to reinforce those new skills.

As an example, most salespeople will approach a client with the phrase "May I help you?" even though they may have learned from sales training that phrase is completely ineffectual. Why? The answer is usually either "No" or "Can you get me…." They tend to fall back into old, comfortable behaviors that lead to the most common, easiest skills and do not move the sales process forward or uncover needs.

SOLUTION:

Sales training must include practical behaviors, not just knowledge, about what makes sales.

Salespeople need to change their behavior patterns. Training is only effective if it teaches small, concrete steps to be taken. These steps must be practiced and monitored thoroughly and consistently over time with constant reinforcement. Take one step at a time. Rather than try to cover everything at once, work on a sequence of steps.

That's why when I work with an organization, it is focused on real-time, experiential processes and broken down step by step to ensure optimal results. Small changes are easier and have more "stick" factors. Along with reinforcement, it provides lasting results.

You wouldn't expect to go to the gym once for optimal results, right? Or for the trainer to say you have to increase your exercise without a step-by-step plan. Why would we expect sellers to increase sales without that step-by-step plan and reinforcement?

For example, the first step should typically be ensuring every single client who enters the showroom is greeted properly so the clients enjoy the experience. Using a phrase like, "What brings you in today?" instead of "May I help you?" becomes a much more effective sales question. It immediately feels more conversational and not quite so cliché. It solicits more information from the client and will lead to a more productive (and hopefully profitable) interaction.

They can take an active interest in the client's situation and individual wishes. Seek to uncover *all* of the needs, not just what they came in for. This was once called "up-selling," but now it's considered the sales process. There's a huge difference between wanting to sell and genuinely being interested in the client's needs. Using this technique, the message comes across clearly.

"Given a 10% **chance** of a 100 times payoff, you should take that bet every time".

-Jeff Bezos

6

Owners do not measure the viability of lines and do not measure how much each line is making per square foot.

We are not a retail industry, but some things need to parrot what a retail space does well, and that is to get a big value from floor-space.

Multi-line showrooms carry anywhere from 10 to more than 70 lines. It is impossible to give enough attention to each line. Therefore, as a showroom, finding out which lines are the most sellable with the least amount of follow-up and problems is imperative. This information should then be communicated through sales goals and space on the floor as to which lines deserve the most attention.

In business terms, it's known as Return on Investment (ROI). Successful companies all know they must get 2 – 3 times the return on their investment. The investment includes time, effort, and square footage, not just top-line money.

Selling a line that takes up too much of the seller's time is not an effective way to run a profitable showroom. We always say, "Time is money," for a reason; IT IS!

One of the first things I did as the manager of a multi-line show-room was to assess what lines were actually making money. This involved reviewing criteria such as:

- Good customer service
- Good lead times
- Limited mistakes
- Limited quality problems
- Good sales tools
- Ability to work openly with the individual showrooms
- Open to territory-specific floor sampling
- Marketability of the product
- Being represented in all territories, not limited to some

This data should all be analyzed, and the companies who scored the best should be the ones who met most of the criteria and were given the most floor space. This was then communicated to the salespeople, and everyone knew exactly what lines they needed to concentrate on to make each hour of sales time most effective regarding profitability. There was NO guessing, haphazard thinking or even taking the easiest way out that could waste time.

Notice that absolutely, at no time did we include information on how big the line was or what kind of name it had in the industry. If a manufacturer does not maintain its partnership by meeting most of these criteria, it won't help profitability. It will erode it.

When problems and mistakes occur with a line, the clients blame the showroom! They are disappointed, which affects the relationship with the showroom, and salespeople have to spend far too much time on follow-up and mending fences.

So, how can you run a profitable showroom if you do not measure how much money you earn per square foot? The answer is you can't. Many showrooms do not take this measure because they focus on HOW the showroom looks instead of how it works– and what lines actually make it money without costly issues.

SOLUTION:

Showrooms must prioritize lines that actually make the most money.

If you take the time to look at sales vs. space and focus on those lines, I guarantee your showroom will gain much more momentum and profitability. Although initially, it takes time, the payback in profitability is incredible.

It's not just about the beauty of the products or the name on the product; the question should be, "Is this line not only making money, but is it profitable?" It's very expensive to run a showroom. Every square foot should be making as much money as possible.

In a perfect world, showrooms would drop the least profitable lines and cause the most problems for salespeople and clients. However, if there is a reluctance to eliminate those lines from the floor, be sure to always communicate to the sellers *not* to push those lines more than the ones identified as most profitable.

"More is not better. Better is better. You don't need more stuff; you need stuff you'll actually use."

-Alex Steffen

7

Showrooms make the mistake of assuming adding more lines will generate more profits.

With numerous showrooms closing, more and more lines are looking for homes. Several showrooms are falsely lured into thinking that featuring additional lines will translate into more profitability. That is the farthest thing from the truth.

Adding a new line and keeping all of the existing lines just crowds a showroom with low-performing lines. If a new line is added, then it is critical that you drop an existing line with poor results from the showroom. Only then does it make sense to add a new line in hopes of covering those losses and gaining more market share.

Adding new lines also splits the time a salesperson has to sell other lines. Sometimes showing low-performing lines requires so much time that more viable lines suffer, resulting in low or no sales. This reinforces the myth that busyness equals business! Again, just because a salesperson is extremely busy showing multiple lines and products, this does not mean they are actually making more sales.

How often have you heard from a salesperson, "Boy, I am just swamped!" I would question whether that busy salesperson is actually making sales and generating profitability, or if they are stuck rolling around in a hamster wheel due to low-performing lines that take a lot of their time and don't produce results.

As well, higher-performing lines, when sales are jeopardized by salespeople spending time on low-performing lines, end up leaving a showroom sometimes causing undo stress on the profitability of the showroom.

There are only so many hours in a selling day. No matter how hard we try, we can't change that. Adding more lines takes time away from existing lines. If some of those existing lines are easier to sell, it only makes sense that the showroom can be more successful and profitable to focus exclusively on those lines; digging deeper, not wider. It is a mistake to divert time and attention from those lines just to have more selections for a client. Again, when running a successful showroom, more is *not* more! Adding more lines can do more harm than good.

SOLUTION:

Streamline your lines!

The truth is that less is more. Selling deeper, not wider, makes a much more profitable showroom. Fewer, really good lines can make much more profit than too many low-performing, time-sucking lines that take up precious resources.

We must always remember: Showrooms are sales organizations, not product companies. And taking on more lines can increase sales, but are they increasing profitability or just another false sense of security? So what is the answer to a suffering showroom business? It's not just adding more lines and thinking that's the answer. It may not be as difficult as it sounds. Sure, it will take change, and change is not always easy, but the alternative is much worse.

The design center business is down. Showroom managers may need to be properly trained to treat the showroom as a sales organization. Some salespeople and managers are bogged down with "busy" to even think about a sales strategy and training.

Therefore, they would be much more effective and profitable by looking at the internal structure and training on effective strategies for management and salespeople along with the aforementioned showroom audit. This will result in a well-oiled sales organization. If showrooms rely on the momentum of particular lines or add more lines for their sales, the design business won't thrive in this or any economy.

CASE STUDY

When I became the manager of a large, multi-line showroom, I faced a showroom that still hadn't been profitable since it opened. It represented a whopping 62 lines. I immediately assessed every single line and came up with only six lines giving us the greatest return on investment.

I instructed the salespeople to focus on those lines to drive up sales and, in turn, profitability. In less than a year, the showroom became profitable. Salespeople were, for the first time, earning commission checks. In two years, sales increased by almost $5 million. Designers came in more often because we sold them lines that caused the fewest problems. That is value!

The salespeople were also freed up to take care of clients in the showroom rather than endlessly being on the phone following up on orders. Instead, they could follow up on quotations and other tasks that actually produce sales. They proactively greeted every client who came into the showroom. Gone were the days of a client in pursuit of an available salesperson, as often happens in showrooms.

Not only did we sell two and sometimes three times as much of the lines that provided us with the needed support and that generated the best results, but it had a huge impact on the profitability of our showroom and the sellers made more money in less time!

Notes

"If it falls your lot to be a street sweeper, go out and sweep streets like Michelangelo painted pictures.

-Martin Luther King, Jr.

BONUS

Everyone working in a showroom is a salesperson no matter what their job description. They should be taught to go above and beyond and have fun doing it!

I discovered, by chance, that everyone needs to be a salesperson in order to keep Operating Expenses down and profitability up. When you're hiring, sales should always be a part of the interviewing process.

When I was a Regional Sales Director, I overheard the sales assistant to one of my outside sellers talking to a client. After conducting the business at hand (finding out when the order was to be delivered), she kindly asked "Is there was anything else she might need <u>on this project?</u>"

I then heard her say, "Oh yes, we have fabric that would be great for draperies in that bedroom. What, more specifically, are you looking for?"

It ended up in another sale that the salesperson did not even know about at that time or generate, but his sales assistant did.

The lesson learned is everyone needs to be a part of sales training. When you're looking at a budget, every sales counts! When your looking at profit, every employee needs to go above and beyond what they were originally hired for. They need to learn how to sell to increase sales at every opportunity, even checking on an existing order!

Closing Thoughts

Where would we be without designers? It's imperative that the motivation behind all of our sales strategies is to make the designers happy. Our job is to help them help their clients.

We need to continue to rely on designers coming to showrooms and emailing or calling to do business, as well as think beyond that as our sole business model.

Some of us can remember when we used business cards and catalogs. We wanted to get "real estate" in design firms by putting all our wares on their shelves. More was better. Sample, sample, sample.

The thinking was, "if it's not there, they will not buy."

That may have been true in 1987 (which I don't believe was the truth even then), but it's certainly not true anymore. The landscape has changed completely.

We need to look to the future of selling and showrooms. Meet designers where they are. That means using technology, amongst other business strategies, to increase sales viability.

What are our demographics, and are they changing? If so, how are we addressing that? We are very lucky that, when writing this book, most designers are still between 45 and 60. This is not about ageism. It's about looking at the current AND future demographics. Who— and how—will we lead the industry into the future?

Additionally, as the demographics of designers are changing, there's the elusive HENRY (high earner, not rich yet) that is now becoming a buyer. There are more generations in the workforce than ever before. Those demographics are getting younger, and there are more and different ways to get to these buyers and designers. How do we reel them in?

Some showrooms think it's going retail. Someday that might be the case, but for now can we do things differently to preserve the to-the-trade showroom by using more technology and meeting a younger audience where they are and doing what they do?

I say unequivocally: YES!

Let's make it easier for those who want to buy products online to buy online from us. Let's have a digital division, sink more money into technology, and away from drowning in new product expenses, where trained professionals can sell in-stock or made-to-order products online to trained designers. Let's make it easier to reach a wider audience, meet them where they are, and sell to them!

There will always be a human element in sales. At least, I hope so. As artificial intelligence (AI) improves, people will still need to be included in the human experience. Sellers will always be a huge part of sales. AI cannot yet develop relationships; only humans can. Yes, we work in a very tactile industry. But can we widen our thinking?

It's not about throwing the baby out with the bathwater. It's about always looking to the future, identifying the challenges, and adapting in effective ways.

SHOWROOMS CAN'T AFFORD TO WAIT. THE TIME FOR CHANGE IS NOW.

Successful businesses are always re-inventing themselves. It's not that leading businesses have not made mistakes; quite the opposite, in fact. The difference is they take calculated risks; if it doesn't work, they learn from those errors and begin thinking and operating differently.

In a Harvard Business Review article by David Sull about the near fatality of IBM, he stated the worst mistake IBM made back in the 1980s was that they didn't change with the times. He cited that the most prevalent reason for business failures was just sticking to what companies know or what has worked in the past. He called this *"active inertia"* and insightfully explained: "Active inertia exists because the pull of the past is so strong." IBM did not believe personal computers were important in the computer business and buried their heads in the sand. Holding onto their old beliefs almost put them out of business. The lessons of this article, written in 1999, could not be more true today, nearly 25 years later.

Unfortunately, there are many examples of companies that didn't change with the times, including Blockbuster and Borders Bookstores, to name a couple. We don't want the showroom industry to be next.

Buying habits have changed, and the design world needs to address those changes. Let's not continue to be myopic and think we know best. If we go along with the status quo, we may see the demise of the showroom. Many have already suffered or shut down completely.

Owners and showroom staff must change their 20th-century thinking and look into new policies and technologies to move them into the 21st century and beyond.

The solution is to become a more modern version of an old business model. Just like design styles change over time, so should our showroom operations.

Showrooms can be saved. They can become more profitable.

It requires only a few changes to our thinking about how a showroom runs, its purpose, and how it can best serve our clients.

If you remember only one thing, remember this:

It's not about the product or even the place the product lives in; it's about smart business decisions.

Keep your eyes open for my next book on how to incorporate the GUSTO system into my Master Class: 7 Core Principles to Optimize Sales.

About the Author

Deborah Flate
Author, Speaker, & Salesaccelerator
Specializing in the *Interior Design Product* and *Showroom Sectors*

Deborah's remarkable career spans over two decades in sales and sales management, during which she has collaborated with the best showrooms in the industry. Her training programs, workshops, books, articles, videos, and keynote speeches have revolutionized the selling approach of countless salespeople, cementing her success in the field.

By leveraging the 7 Core Principles of Optimized Selling and the GUSTO system, she introduces a distinctive approach that reinvents sales strategies. These tools become invaluable assets, empowering sellers to elevate their sales skills and master time management efficiently.

She offers expert guidance to premier showrooms, product companies, and executives across the country, empowering them to enhance customer experience and strategic account management. Her invaluable insights enable the creation of high-performing sales teams.

To enrich your sales team's performance or to invite her as a speaker for your next sales meeting, you can contact her by emailing:

deborah@dialogue-consulting.com

Reach out now to explore the valuable opportunities she can bring to your organization.

> "If you're results-oriented and want to solve the challenges you're facing, you should hire Deborah. She is focused, enjoys the process, and delivers".
>
> *-President of major luxury showroom*